# Ecosystems

# Temperate Forests

## Greg Reid

CHELSEA
CLUBHOUSE

An Imprint of Chelsea House Publishers
A Haights Cross Communications Company
**Philadelphia**

To Mary-Anne, Julian and Damian

This edition first published in 2004 in the United States of America by Chelsea Clubhouse, a division of Chelsea House Publishers and a subsidiary of Haights Cross Communications.

Chelsea Clubhouse
1974 Sproul Road, Suite 400
Broomall, PA 19008-0914

The Chelsea House world wide web address is www.chelseahouse.com

Library of Congress Cataloging-in-Publication Data Applied for.

ISBN 0-7910-7942-2

First published in 2004 by
MACMILLAN EDUCATION AUSTRALIA PTY LTD
627 Chapel Street, South Yarra, Australia, 3141

Associated companies and representatives throughout the world.

Copyright © Greg Reid 2004

Copyright in photographs © individual photographers as credited

Edited by Anna Fern and Miriana Dasovic
Text and cover design by Polar Design
Illustrations and maps by Alan Laver, Shelly Communications
Photo research by Legend Images

Printed in China

## Acknowledgments

The author and publisher are grateful to the following for permission to reproduce copyright material:

Cover photograph: an American black bear in a temperate forest, courtesy of Photodisc.

Otto Rogge/ANTphoto.com.au, p. 27 (top); Silvestris/ANTphoto.com.au, p. 9 (top left); Erwin & Peggy Bauer/Auscape International, p. 15 (center left & right); Davo Blair/Auscape International, p. 19 (top left); Jean-Paul Ferrero/Auscape International, pp. 16 (bottom), 18; Hellio-Van Ingen/Auscape International, p. 13 (right); Colin Monteath/Auscape International, p. 22; John Shaw/Auscape International, p. 9 (bottom left); Australian Picture Library/Corbis, pp. 19 (top center), 20; Corbis Digital Stock, pp. 3 (top & center), 5, 6, 7 (left), 10 (left), 16 (top), 19 (bottom), 31, 32; Getty Images/Photodisc Blue, p. 14 (right); Jiri Lochman/Lochman Transparencies, pp. 12, 15 (top center), 17 (top left & right); Pelusey Photography, pp. 7 (right), 13 (top left), 23; Photodisc, pp. 3 (bottom), 8, 9 (top right & bottom right), 10 (right), 11, 13 (bottom), 14 (left), 15 (top left & bottom), 17 (bottom), 19 (top right), 24, 25 (bottom), 30 (both); Photolibrary.com, p. 28; Photolibrary.com/Index Stock, p. 27 (bottom); Reuters, pp. 21, 25, 26, 29 (both); The G.R. "Dick" Roberts Photo Library, p. 13 (top center).

page 5 graph statistics extracted from *State of the World's Forests*, Food and Agricultural Organisation of the United Nations, 2001—Appendix 3: Global tables (Table 3 Forest Cover 2000 and Table 14 Distribution of total forest cover by ecological zone)

While every care has been taken to trace and acknowledge copyright, the publisher tenders their apologies for any accidental infringement where copyright has proved untraceable. Where the attempt has been unsuccessful, the publisher welcomes information that would redress the situation.

**Please note**
At the time of printing, the Internet addresses appearing in this book were correct. Owing to the dynamic nature of the Internet, however, we cannot guarantee that all these addresses will remain correct.

The author would like to thank Anatta Abrahams, Janine Hanna, Eulalie O'Keefe, Kerry Regan, Marcia Reid.

# Contents

When a word is printed in **bold**, you can look up
its meaning in the Glossary on page 31.

# What Are Temperate Forests

A temperate forest environment is part of an ecosystem. An ecosystem is made up of living plants and animals and their non-living environment of air, water, energy, and nutrients.

Temperate forests are more than just forests with beautiful reds and golds in the fall. These colorful forests are temperate **deciduous** forests, but they are only one type of temperate forest. Each type of temperate forest is named after the main type of tree found there. Temperate deciduous forests have deciduous trees, such as oaks, which are bare in winter.

Temperate coniferous forests have **conifers**, such as spruce. These trees are **evergreen**. They do not lose their needle-like leaves in one season. Some temperate forests have deciduous and coniferous trees together.

In Australia, some temperate forests have evergreen **eucalyptus** trees, such as blue gum. Temperate rain forests also have evergreen trees, such as southern beech, as well as conifers, such as the Huon pine. There is a great variety of temperate forests.

Temperate forests are found in temperate regions of the world, between the Tropics and the poles.

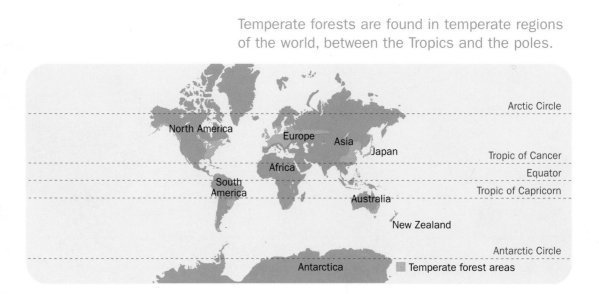

North America

Europe

Asia

Japan

Africa

South America

Australia

New Zealand

Antarctica

Arctic Circle

Tropic of Cancer

Equator

Tropic of Capricorn

Antarctic Circle

Temperate forest areas

# Where Do Temperate Forests Grow?

Temperate forests grow on every continent except Antarctica. Temperate forests grow in temperate regions of the world, between the Tropics and the poles. They make up 26 percent of the forested area of the world.

The largest areas of temperate forest are found in the northern half of the world, or Northern Hemisphere, south of the taiga (northern coniferous forests). These large areas include western and central Europe, eastern North America, eastern China, Korea, and Japan. Smaller areas of forest grow in Mexico and Central America.

**Ecofact**

## Shrinking Temperate Forests

Once, temperate forests covered much greater areas of Earth's land surface. Today, they cover only 9.7 percent, because large areas have been cleared by humans.

In the southern half of the world, or Southern Hemisphere, smaller areas of temperate forests grow in parts of South America, southern Africa, southern Australia, and New Zealand. Most temperate forests have been cleared for timber and farmland.

A Northern Hemisphere forest in the fall

Where temperate forests are found

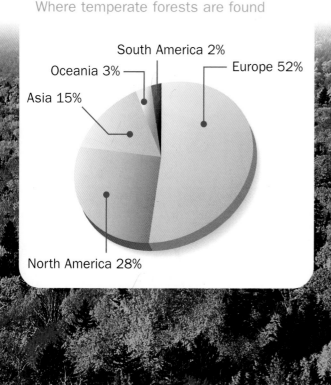

South America 2%

Oceania 3%

Europe 52%

Asia 15%

North America 28%

5

# Types of Temperate Forests

The climate, soils, plants, and animals in temperate forests can vary by location and elevation, or height above sea level.

## Temperate Deciduous Forests

Temperate deciduous forests grow best in areas with fertile soils and a mild climate. Most trees, such as oak, beech, chestnut, and ash, have broad leaves which they shed at the end of the growing season.

## Temperate Coniferous Forests

Temperate coniferous forests sometimes grow in areas with poor soil, such as mountains. They also grow in areas with less rainfall than temperate deciduous forests.

## Temperate Mixed Forests

Temperate mixed forests have conifers, deciduous trees, and evergreen trees. In the Northern Hemisphere, where the taiga forests end, willows, poplars, and birches begin to appear among the conifers. Temperate mixed forests in the Southern Hemisphere have conifers and evergreen trees, such as southern beech and chinquapin.

A temperate coniferous forest in North America

# Temperate Eucalyptus Forests

Most of the temperate forests in Australia have tall eucalyptus trees, with small trees, shrubs, and tree ferns underneath. There are some 600 species of eucalyptus found in Australia and nearby islands. Many eucalyptus trees are able to survive frequent bushfires, and some trees need the bushfires to open their seeds.

# Temperate Rain Forests

Temperate rain forests are found on the western coast of continents with high rainfall. They usually grow in mountainous areas near the sea. These forests have many types of conifers. Temperate rain forests are rare and once covered about 0.2 percent of Earth's land area. These forests have the largest trees in the world.

Temperate eucalyptus forest in Western Australia

## Ecofact

### Tree Giants

Giant trees are common in the temperate rain forests of North America. Redwoods reach 365 feet (110 meters), Douglas firs 330 feet (100 meters), Sitka spruce 315 feet (95 meters), giant sequoia 310 feet (94 meters) and Western hemlock 260 feet (79 meters).

A Californian redwood forest

# Temperate Forest Climate

**T**emperate forests are found in areas where there is enough **precipitation** for trees to grow. The forests receive about 30 to 60 inches (750 to 1,500 millimeters) of precipitation, spread fairly evenly throughout the year. In winter, the cold soil temperatures stop deciduous temperate forest trees from taking up water.

Temperate forests grow in moderate climates with four different seasons. The temperature varies widely from season to season. Summers are warm, with temperatures around 64 degrees Fahrenheit (18 degrees Celsius). Winters are cool to cold, with temperatures around 37 degrees Fahrenheit (3 degrees Celsius). Winters last between two to six months. The average yearly temperature is about 48 degrees Fahrenheit (10 degrees Celsius). Temperate forests grow in areas with a long growing season of about six months (140 to 200 days). The growing season has four to six frost-free months.

## Ecofact

### Spring Flowers

Many small trees, shrubs, herbs, and plants on the floor of temperate forests have adapted to flower in spring, before the deciduous trees are in full leaf.

Winters in temperate forests are very cold. The deciduous trees are bare.

8

# Seasonal Cycle of Temperate Deciduous Forests

Temperate deciduous forests have a seasonal cycle with four stages. The growing season is in spring and summer. In the warm summer, the broad green leaves of the trees catch sunlight to make food for the plants to grow. In the cool fall, the leaves of the trees change color and fall.

In the cold winter, deciduous trees are **dormant**. They save energy by not growing when light and water are scarce. In spring, when it is warmer, new green leaf buds start to appear on the trees. In order to survive, plants and animals have to adapt to the changing seasons.

Summer → Fall

Seasons in temperate deciduous forests

Spring ← Winter

# Temperate Deciduous Forests

Temperate deciduous forests have three layers of life. There are many open spaces between the canopies of the large trees, so sunlight is able to reach the lower layers. These three layers provide a good **habitat** for the animals that live there.

Layers in a temperate deciduous forest

**Canopy**
Large trees, such as oak, maple, walnut, beech, elm, hickory, chestnut, liquidambar, and basswood, form a dense canopy in summer.

**Understory**
In the thick undergrowth there are small trees and shrubs, such as mountain laurels, azaleas, huckleberries, and rhododendrons.

**Forest floor**
Here there are lichens, mosses, herbs, and small plants, such as European bluebells and hepaticas.

## Ecofact

# Salamanders

**Amphibians** called salamanders live in the leaf litter on the forest floor in some temperate forests in North America and Europe. The tadpoles of these animals live in small ponds on the forest floor.

European mountain salamander

# Temperate Deciduous Forest Food Chain

Oak trees and the animals connected in this food chain are found in temperate deciduous forests of Europe, Asia, and North America.

Oak tree gets its energy from the Sun, and nutrients from soil and decaying matter on the forest floor.

**1** →

Earthworm (decomposer) breaks down the leaves of the oak tree.

**2** →

**6** ↑ Oak tree takes up soil nutrients.

Temperate deciduous forest food chain

**3** ↙

**5** ↑ Fox dies and is broken down by worms and bacteria (decomposers). The nutrients are returned to the soil.

Woodcock (**insectivore**) eats the earthworm.

← **4**

Fox (carnivore) eats the woodcock.

# Temperate Coniferous and Mixed Forests

Many of the animals that live in temperate coniferous and mixed forests also live in temperate deciduous forests. Herbivorous insects, such as tent caterpillars and spruce budworms, sometimes eat all the leaves on conifers and deciduous trees.

Many birds are insectivores and migrate during winter when there are no insects. A few, such as jays, woodpeckers, crows, and ravens, and **birds of prey**, such as owls, hawks, eagles, and falcons, stay in temperate coniferous and temperate mixed forests all year round.

There are many small mammals, such as hares, squirrels, mice, possums, and voles. Carnivores, such as wildcats, martens, weasels, and birds of prey, hunt these animals. Large carnivores include bears, wolves, bobcats, clouded leopards, and mountain lions.

American black bear

# Temperate Mixed Forest Food Chain

In temperate mixed forests, there are many plants and animals connected in food chains. Here is an example of a food chain from a temperate mixed forest in south-west China.

Grasses and herbs get their energy from the Sun, and nutrients from soil and decaying matter on the forest floor.

**2** An insect, such as a grasshopper (herbivore), eats the grasses and herbs.

**1** →

Temperate mixed forest food chain in south-west China

**3** Golden pheasant (insectivore) eats the grasshopper.

**6** Grasses and herbs take up soil nutrients.

**5** Clouded leopard dies and is broken down by worms and bacteria (decomposers). The nutrients are returned to the soil.

**4** ←

Clouded leopard (carnivore) eats the golden pheasant.

## Ecofact

### Giant Panda

The **endangered** giant panda lives in temperate mixed forests in China, where it feeds on bamboo in the understory. It is the symbol of the World Wildlife Fund (WWF) conservation group.

Giant panda

# Temperate Eucalyptus Forests

Animals that live in temperate eucalyptus forests have made many **adaptations** to survive. Many creatures, such as insects, possums, and parrots, eat eucalyptus leaves, flowers, and seeds. Eucalyptus leaves are poisonous to other animals because of the oils they contain. Australian parrots, such as rainbow lorikeets, are colorful so they can easily hide in the trees. Wombats are the largest burrowing **marsupials**. They sleep during the day in their burrows and feed at night on roots and plants.

Sugar gliders and yellow-bellied gliders have webbed skin between their legs. They feed at night on insects and the nectar, sap, and seeds of eucalyptus trees. They can glide more than 165 feet (50 meters) between trees to find food or escape from predators, such as the spotted-tailed quoll. There are many links between eucalyptus forest plants and animals.

The sugar glider is a type of possum that lives in Australian eucalypt forests.

## Koalas

Koalas are not bears, but tree-living marsupials. They only eat the leaves of some eucalyptus trees, and do not need to drink water. The habitat of these endangered animals is being cleared in many areas for farming and cities.

Koala

16

# Temperate Eucalyptus Forest Food Chain

In temperate eucalyptus forests, many plants and animals are connected in food chains. Here is an example of a food chain from temperate eucalyptus forests in Tasmania.

Tasmanian blue gum gets its energy from the Sun, and nutrients from soil and decaying matter on the forest floor.

Common brushtail possum (herbivore) eats the flowers and leaves of the Tasmanian blue gum.

Temperate eucalyptus forest food chain in Tasmania, Australia

**5** Tasmanian blue gum takes up soil nutrients.

**4** Tasmanian devil dies and is broken down by worms and bacteria (decomposers). The nutrients are returned to the soil.

**3** Tasmanian devil (carnivore) eats the common brushtail possum.

# Temperate Rain Forests

Temperate rain forests grow in areas of high rainfall between mountain ranges and the ocean. New Zealand, south-eastern Australia, Tasmania, southern Chile and Argentina, Japan, and the north-west coast of North America have temperate rain forests.

There are fewer types of plants and animals in temperate rain forests compared with tropical rain forests. Sometimes, temperate rain forests contain only one or two main types of tree, such as the giant sequoias of North America, which are the largest living things on land. The main types of tree in many areas are conifers, which are also called firs and pines. Trees are often covered in orchids, ferns, and other plants.

Temperate rain forest in New Zealand's South Island

# Temperate Rain Forest Food Chain

In temperate rain forests, many plants and animals are connected in food chains. Here is an example of a food chain from temperate rain forests in North America.

Douglas fir gets its energy from the Sun, and nutrients from soil and decaying matter on the forest floor.

**1 →**

Douglas squirrel (herbivore) eats the seeds of the Douglas fir.

**2**

Temperate rain forest food chain in North America

**5**

Douglas fir takes up soil nutrients.

**3**

**4**

Northern spotted owl dies and is broken down by worms and bacteria (decomposers). The nutrients are returned to the soil.

Northern spotted owl (carnivore) eats the Douglas squirrel.

## Ecofact

# Fish in the Forest

Pacific salmon are an important part of some temperate rain forest food chains in North America. The salmon return to the same stream where they were born to lay their eggs and die. Many animals, including bears, eat the salmon.

A bear hunting salmon

# Indigenous Peoples

**Indigenous peoples** have lived in temperate forests for thousands of years, mainly in small groups. They harvested a wide variety of things from the forest without harming the ecosystem.

The Cherokee Indians of south-eastern United States once hunted animals and gathered food in temperate forests, and grew crops in forest clearings. The First Nation peoples of the Pacific coast of North America had large settlements in the temperate rain forests.

In Australia, many Aboriginal groups lived in temperate eucalyptus forests. In New Zealand, the Maori lived in temperate forests. Today, very few indigenous peoples live in temperate forests because many forests have been cleared for timber, farming, and cities.

## Ecofact

### Rich Forests

North America's temperate rain forests have more than 30 tree species and about 250 species of birds and mammals. The forests had several hundred thousand indigenous people before European settlement. There were 60 different languages spoken from Alaska to California.

A Yakima Indian nets a salmon in the traditional way on the Klickitat River, Washington. Many indigenous peoples have hunting rights in their traditional land.

# Indigenous Peoples in Asia and South America

Some indigenous peoples still follow a traditional way of life in temperate forests today. In Asia, there are several indigenous groups still living in temperate forests. Near the Pacific coast of Russia, the Udege and the Nanai people live in temperate mixed forests. They hunt animals and gather forest foods, products, and medicines.

In South America, more than half a million indigenous peoples live in the temperate forests of southern and central Chile. Some of these indigenous peoples still gather plants and hunt the animals in the temperate forests of Chile. Large numbers of South American plant and animal species, such as Pudú deer and Chilote fox, are found nowhere else. The way of life of indigenous peoples in Chile is under threat because of logging, farming, and tree plantations.

These Mapuche Indians in Santiago, Chile, are carrying out a ritual to welcome the new year held on June 21.

# Temperate Forest Resources

Temperate forests supply many valuable things for people. Hardwood timber from deciduous trees, such as oak and beech, is used for furniture and building. Softwood timber from conifers is used for paper pulp and building.

Many garden plants, such as azaleas and rhododendrons, are found in temperate forests. The ancestors of apples, pears, plums, and cherries originally came from temperate forests. These wild plants are more resistant to diseases than **domesticated plants**. Scientists can crossbreed these wild plants with the domestic ones to produce better plants.

Many berries, such as cranberries, blackberries, and raspberries, also originally came from temperate forests. Hazelnuts, walnuts, pecans, mushrooms, truffles, and honey are also found in temperate forests.

Wild rhododendron trees in Bhutan, near the Himalaya Mountains

## Ecofact

### Maple Syrup

There are more than 13 species of maple trees in North American temperate forests. The sap from some sugar maples is tapped from drill holes in the trunk. It is boiled to make maple syrup. A maple leaf is shown on the Canadian flag.

# Nature's Medicine Chest

Temperate forests have many plants that are useful as medicines. Traditional Chinese medicine uses the roots, berries, leaves, and bark of many plants from temperate forests.

Traditional Western herbal medicine also uses many plants from temperate forests. Ginkgo biloba, also called the maidenhair tree, is used as a herb to help memory. A chemical from the bark of the rare Pacific yew tree is used to treat cancer. Aspirin comes from the bark of willow trees. There may be many undiscovered medicines in temperate forests. If temperate forests are cleared for timber and farming, future sources of medicines will be lost forever.

## Ecofact

### The Good Oil

Eucalyptus oil, from the leaves of some eucalyptus trees in temperate eucalyptus forests, is used as a medicine and to kill germs. Eucalyptus oil is used to flavor lozenges, which help to soothe a sore throat.

A traditional Chinese herbal medicine shop

# Threats to Temperate Forests

There are many threats to temperate forests. Natural threats include fires and damage from tornadoes and thunderstorm winds. Threats to forests from human activities include air pollution and the building of roads, cities, mines, and dams.

Temperate forests once covered much larger areas than they do today. In the past, many forests were cleared for farming. However, the biggest threat to temperate forests today is clearing for paper pulp and timber. In some countries, such as Russia, illegal logging is a serious threat to temperate forests.

Once temperate forests are cleared, the area is often replanted with tree plantations. Not as many animals can live in these plantation forests because there is usually only one species of tree. Many temperate forest animals need a variety of tree species to survive.

## Ecofact

### Tree Farms

More than 95 percent of the original deciduous forests in North America have been cleared for timber, farming, and cities. Today, many areas are planted with tree plantations, growing trees for pulpwood, timber, or Christmas trees.

Forest clearing is a threat to many species of plants and animals.

# Threatened Plants and Animals

Temperate forest plants and animals are under threat from different sources. Introduced pests, such as fungi and insects, kill some tree species. Native trees have little resistance to pests from outside areas. In North America, fungi have killed many large elms and American chestnuts. Gypsy moths and maple thrips have also killed large areas of temperate forests.

Animals are under threat from reduced habitat and hunting by people. Many large animals, such as the European wood bison, cannot survive in small areas of forest. In many areas, people have killed large carnivores, such as bears, wolves, and mountain lions, because they eat domestic animals. Eight species of wolf, including the black Florida wolf, are extinct in North America. Two species of wolf are extinct in Japan. More needs to be done to protect threatened plants and animals so they do not become extinct.

In North America, wolves have been hunted to the point of extinction.

# Effects of Clearing Temperate Forests

Temperate forests act like a giant sponge and help to control flooding. They also protect soils from being washed away. When the forests are cleared, flooding and soil **erosion** become problems. The Chinese government has now stopped the cutting of old temperate forests in the Yangtze Valley in order to prevent serious flooding and loss of life.

Temperate forests also help to control the world's climate by absorbing carbon dioxide and releasing oxygen. When temperate forests are cleared, the climate of the whole planet is affected. Rainfall patterns change once forests are cleared.

Temperate forest trees store carbon and help prevent global warming. When trees are burned, carbon dioxide is released into the air. This adds to global warming, which may cause changes to climates all over the world. There are many serious impacts of clearing temperate forests.

## Ecofact

### Chinese Floods

The area draining the Yangtze River has lost 85 percent of its original temperate forest cover. Logging was blamed for the 1998 floods that killed more than 3,000 people and caused more than $20 billion in damage.

An elderly man paddles a wooden wash basin past houses submerged in floodwaters from the Yangtze River in 1998.

# Ecotourism in Temperate Forests

Ecotourism is when visitors pay to see the beauty of a natural ecosystem. People want to visit temperate forests because they were the original ecosystems where most of the world's population now lives. They also are places of great beauty.

Ecotourism does not cause much disturbance to the temperate forests. In many areas, governments and local people can earn more money from people visiting temperate forests than from clearing them. In many countries with temperate forests, such as the United States and Australia, ecotourism is growing in importance. Indigenous people can become guides, showing visitors temperate forest plants and animals. Ecotourism can help protect some valuable temperate forest areas for the future.

Ecotourists hiking in a North American forest

## Ecotourism in Tasmania

The ancient temperate rain forests on the west coast of Tasmania attract thousands of ecotourists each year. People leave nothing but footprints and take nothing but photographs and memories.

Southwest National Park, Tasmania

# Protecting Temperate Forests

**M**ore laws are needed to prevent temperate forests from being destroyed. At present, only a small fraction of the world's temperate forests are protected in national parks and reserves. Governments need to do more to save the most important temperate forests areas before it is too late.

Scientists say that at least 10 percent of temperate forests need to be in national parks and reserves so that their plant and animal species can survive. These parks also need to be large enough to allow the temperate forest plants and animals to survive and breed. People and governments around the world need to be aware of the threats to temperate forests and take action to preserve what is left.

National parks help temperate forest species to survive.

## Ecofact

### Great Smoky Mountains

The Great Smoky Mountains of the United States have a wide variety of temperate forest plants and animals. The area has been declared a World Biosphere Reserve to help protect the rich ecosystem.

# Conservation Groups

International conservation groups, such as the World Wildlife Fund (WWF) and Greenpeace, also help to protect temperate forests. They let many people know about the problems faced by temperate forests, including illegal logging. Sometimes, these groups protest against forest clearing and logging and get the attention of the media.

Some conservation groups buy land for temperate forest reserves. They organize scientists to investigate and write reports on the special features of temperate forest areas. Conservation groups also pressure governments to set up reserves and pass laws to protect unique plants and animals. International agreements have been made to stop the illegal trade in endangered animals.

Greenpeace activists staging a protest. Their sign says "Only 400 Siberian tigers left. Their forest must not be burned!"

## Protest Ship

The ship *Greenpeace* visits countries with some of the largest forests in the world—Russia, Canada, and Brazil. Members of Greenpeace protest against destructive logging and support the indigenous people who are losing their homes.

*Greenpeace*

# How to Save Temperate Forests

**We can all work to save temperate forests.** You can learn more about the importance of temperate forests to the world. Join a conservation group and let others know about the threats to temperate forests. Do not buy items made from old temperate forest woods. Use products made from plantation timber instead. Write to the government and ask them to help save the world's temperate forests.

ecosystems

**The following web sites give more information on temperate forests.**

**Deciduous forest biome**
http://curriculum.calstatela.edu/courses/builders/lessons/less/biomes/deciduous/decfor.html

**Forests**
http://www.ucmp.berkeley.edu/glossary/gloss5/biome/forests.html

**Temperate deciduous forest**
http://www.enchantedlearning.com/biomes/tempdecid/tempdecid.shtml

**Temperate deciduous forest biome**
http://mbgnet.mobot.org/sets/temp/index.htm

**Temperate forest biome**
http://oncampus.richmond.edu/academics/as/education/projects/webunits/biomes/temp.html

# Glossary

| | |
|---|---|
| **adaptations** | changes that help plants and animals survive in an environment |
| **amphibians** | animals that can live on land and in water |
| **birds of prey** | birds, such as eagles and owls, that hunt other animals |
| **camouflage** | when an animal's color or shape help it to blend into the background |
| **conifers** | plants with needle-like leaves and cones |
| **deciduous** | trees that lose their leaves during the coldest parts of the year |
| **decomposers** | organisms, such as worms, fungi, and bacteria, that break down plant and animal matter |
| **domesticated plants** | plants that humans have grown from wild plants |
| **dormant** | period of time in winter when a deciduous tree does not grow |
| **endangered** | in danger of becoming extinct |
| **erosion** | the removal of soil and rocks by wind, water, or ice |
| **eucalyptus** | gum trees from Australia with evergreen, leathery leaves |
| **evergreen** | trees that do not lose their leaves in one season |
| **habitat** | the environment where organisms live |
| **hibernate** | to spend most of the winter asleep |
| **indigenous peoples** | groups of people who first lived in a place, whose traditional ways help them to survive in that place |
| **insectivore** | an animal that eats insects |
| **mammals** | a group of animals that have hair or fur, warm blood, a large brain, and feed their young milk |
| **marsupials** | a group of mammals that carry their young in a pouch |
| **migrate** | to move from one area to another instead of staying in one spot |
| **nocturnal** | animals that come out at night to feed |
| **precipitation** | rain, hail, sleet, or snow falling from the sky |
| **predators** | animals that hunt and eat other animals |
| **scavengers** | animals that live off dead animals |
| **species** | types of plants and animals |

# Index

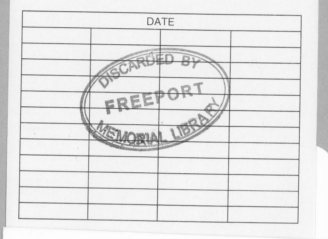